The Missouri Compromise:

AN

ADDRESS

Delivered before the Citizens

OF PITTSFIELD, BY

REV. HEMAN HUMPHREY, D. D..

IN THE BAPTIST CHURCH,

On Sabbath Evening, Feb. 26, 1854.

PITTSFIELD:
REED, HULL & PEIRSON,—PRINTERS,
1854.

REV. H. HUMPHREY, D. D.,

DEAR SIR:

The undersigned, in behalf of a large number of the citizens of this County, respectfully request a copy of your Address on the "Nebraska Bill," for publication.

SAMUEL HARRIS,
CYRUS PRINDLE,
ASA BARR,
} *Committee.*

Pittsfield, March 1, 1854.

GENTLEMEN,

I have received your request in behalf of citizens of this County for a copy of my Address on the Nebraska Bill, now before Congress, and if you think the publication of it will do good it is at your service.

H. HUMPHREY.

Pittsfield, March 1, 1854.

ADDRESS.

FRIENDS OF PUBLIC FAITH AND NATIONAL HONOR:

THERE are times of peril, in the history of every nation, which demand the united counsels and efforts of all the people, to ward off the danger. Sometimes, it is to resist, at every hazard, the invasion of a foreign power; sometimes to quell a formidable insurrection at home; and sometimes, to thwart the stealthy encroachments of wily and aspiring men, who to gain their own selfish purposes, would not hesitate to sacrifice the best interests of the present and of all future generations. Such times of public danger there have been, in the history of this country.

The first, was, in what has since been called the old French war, in 1745, and which was brought to a successful close, by the capture of Quebec, on the heights of Abraham.

The next, and a far more perilous struggle, was in the war of the Revolution, between these then colonies, and the mother country, in which England put forth all her naval and military strength, to coerce submission to her arbitrary laws, and to resist which, required the united efforts and sacrifices of the whole people, during seven long and bloody years. By the blessing of God, on their counsels and their arms, they triumphed, and established their Independence.

No attempt has since been made to conquor us; and if we remain a united people, and keep alive the fire of liberty which glowed in the bosoms of our revolutionary fathers, no power on earth can do it.

Since we became a nation, there have been two cases of open insurrection. I refer to the Shays and Whiskey rebellions, both of which were crushed in the bud, by the energy of the government. Besides these, as you remember, there was danger at one time, that a more formidable insurrection would break out, in one of the oldest states of the Union, and which might have burst forth into a devouring conflagration, if a man of iron nerves and iron will had not been in the Presidential chair.

Since these, I can think of no other outbreak, save the late Erie insurrection, so tenderly nursed, by guardians of the laws, who I am sure never served under General Jackson.

Of the far more dangerous encroachments upon our vital national interests, in a different form, I shall speak directly; and but for these my voice would not have been heard here this evening.

It is said, by some, that ministers of the gospel ought never to meddle with politics. I profess still to be a minister of the gospel, though I have no parochial charge, so that if, on this occasion, I should seem to anybody, to "stretch myself beyond my measure," I shall fall under the same condemnation, as if I had a parish, and I am ready to meet the charge of intermedling with what does not belong to me, in my own behalf, and that of my brethren.

I freely admit that it does not become us to leave our high and sacred calling, and go down into the arena of party politics, and soil the ermine of our profession, by doing battle, on the one side or the other. "The weapons of our warfare are not carnal." As ambassadors of the Prince of peace, we should rather act the part of mediators, and strive to allay the bitterness of crimination, and recrimination, if we cannot reconcile the parties. But to say, that ministers have no right to meddle with politics; not even to go to the polls, as some contend, is to disfranchise them, as they would not even a criminal, after he had served out his time in the state prison.

The eternal principles of right and wrong, of justice and humanity, and religion, are so interwoven with politics, or the science of government, that entirely to eschew POLITICS, in the discharge of their public duties, would be to ignore all those principles, and betray their trust as teachers of morality and religion.

There may be times, there are crises, when it is the duty of ministers of the gospel to plunge into the thickest of politics; to "cry aloud and not spare, to lift up their voices like a trumpet." So thought and so spake our fathers, in the times of the Revolution, "which tried men's souls." It was a mighty struggle for liberty, for the sacred rights of three millions of people, against the encroachments of foreign aggression. The ministers of that day, conferred not with flesh and blood. They were of one heart and one mind. So far as my knowledge extends, there was not a TORY among them. "Sink or swim, live or die," no padlock could have closed their lips. They were determined to be free with the people, or to share and suffer with them in their subjugation; and I am sure you will bear me out in saying, that no class of men, in proportion to their numbers, did more than they did, to achieve our Independence. They preached, they prayed, politics. They encouraged, they exhorted, their people to enlist into the service. When whole companies of militia, the bone and muscle, and stay of their congregations, were called out by those alarms which were so frequent during the war, they met them at the hour of their sudden departure ; encouraged them to go ; exhorted them to fight valiantly for liberty, and implored the God of battles to go with them and shield their heads in the day of slaughter. Yea, there were not wanting examples among them, of buckling on the armor, and shouldering the musket, and marching to the places of alarm and danger. I know in whose presence I say this.

Then it was, that while husbands, and brothers, and sons were in the army, and the angel of death was hovering over the battle fields, hospitals and prison ships, that "the angels of the churches," were going from house to house, visiting the bereaved widows, mothers and fatherless in their afflictions, subsisting as best they could without salaries, and even laboring with their own hands to help their sorrowing people, whose protectors were already slain, or hourly exposed to the shafts which flew so thick and fast around them. Such were the ministers of that day. Such were their prayers and preaching, and exhortations, and sacrifices for liberty. I dare say the British parliament thought, these ministers mingled too much in politics ; and quite sure I am, that no class of our revolutionary fathers were more hated and feared than they. This was before we were born.

But there was, some twenty-five years ago, another

arbitrary encroachment upon the most sacred human rights, against which the ministers of that day felt it their duty solemnly to protest. I allude to the forcible expulsion of the Indians from their home on this side of the Mississippi, in violation of a score of treaties. This was looked upon, by nearly all the people of the north, and justly, I think, as a great national robbery. Regarding it in this light, ministers boldly spoke and preached against it; and for sympathizing with their wronged and defenceless red brothers, whom they were successfully laboring to civilize and christianize, two of the missionaries were incarcerated as felons, at hard labor, in a Georgia prison. I then lifted up my feeble voice against the violation of the most solemn pledges of the government, in a discourse which I entitled INDIAN RIGHTS AND OUR DUTIES, and which was printed, and pretty widely circulated at the time. I could not help remonstrating, with all the power I had. I said then, and I say now, that I had rather receive the blessing of one poor Indian, as he looked back for the last time upon the graves of his fathers, than to sleep under the marble of all the Cæsars.

And now, we have all suddenly reached another crisis, infinitely more alarming, which ought to excite every christian, every patriot, every friend of humanity and justice, to fervent prayer and the most determined opposition. It is no less than a meditated violation of national faith, which would disgrace any European or Asiatic despot, and which, if perpetrated, threatens nothing less, than to rend the Union into fragments, and dig the grave of our boasted liberties. It is nothing less, than to go back THIRTY-FOUR YEARS of our short, but glorious republican history, and annul one of the most solemn compacts that was ever entered into by the Federal government; and that, for the main, if not the sole purpose, of extending the blighting curse of slavery, over a vast free territory, larger than England, Scotland, France, Portugal, and Italy, all put together. And now, what would the men of '76, who fought and periled every thing for liberty, say, if they could return to the country which they baptised with their blood, and left rejoicing under the broad banner of independence? What would they say if they could come back to-morrow, and look over this vast confederation, and go to Washington and listen to the grasping coalition, which now rules the nation? Would they believe their eyes or their ears? And if the ministers of that day, who moved heaven and earth by their prayers and preaching, against the encroachments of the British crown;—what would they say to us, their sons and successors in the sacred office? Would they caution us to beware what WE say, either in the pulpit or out of it, lest we should be charged with meddling with politics? What if that venerable man of God, Rev. Thomas Allen, who sleeps in yonder tomb, could be waked up, and have the Nebraska bill, with its black section, put into his hands, what would HE say? I declare to you, I would not for any price, go and knock at the door of that tomb, if I knew that I would bring him up, except it were in the last extremity of expiring liberty, that he might again buckle on his armor and march up to the cannon's mouth. No; let him sleep, and never, till the day of judgment, know anything of the atrocious conspiracy which has been concocted this winter, at the seat of our government.

This is a crisis, in which we who love our country and bear the sacred office, must speak and will speak. If we "should hold our peace, the stones would immediately cry out." If you could poll, the whole ministry of the free States to-day, you would not find one in a hundred, but that would remonstrate at the top of their voices against the repeal of the Missouri compromise, which declares that from all the territory "purchased of France, lying north of 36 deg. 30 min., slavery and involuntary servitude, otherwise than in the punishment of crimes, shall be, and is hereby FOREVER PROHIBITED."

In speaking to you to-night, I do not claim, with Elihu, to be quite "full of the matter," but I am so near full, that I cannot hold my peace. Though I have now been in the ministry almost fifty years, I have never seen the time, but once, (I allude to the violent expulsion of the Indians,) when the faith, and honor, and justice of the nation were so much in danger of being tarnished, as since the opening of this Congress.

And now, if you will bear with the prolixity of an old man, I will endeavor to sustain the strong language which I have used, in denouncing the Nebraska bill in its present form, so far as I have yet been able to learn, what shape it has, "in member, joint, or limb."

But in order to do this, I must just glance at the history of the first introduction of slavery into this country, and its steady march towards the preponderance which it has gained, and now holds in the national counsels. And here I wish to say, that the slave states are not answerable for the bringing in of this enormous curse and wrong. It was forced upon them by the mother country, against their most earnest remonstrances. Virginia, and I believe one or two of the other colonies would have kept it out if they could; but once introduced, it was not in their power to abolish the trafic, so long as they were under the British crown. From this nefarious source of constant supply, slavery had gained such a foot-hold, before our fathers severed the cord that bound them to the British throne, and hewed out their independence with the sword, that the wisest and most ardent friends of liberty at the south, saw not how the system, which had grown up in spite of them, could at once be abolished; but they hoped and believed, that it would not be permanently fastened upon them. And so far were their most illustrious statesmen, who assisted in framing the Constitution, from wishing to have slavery gain another foot of ground on this continent, that they deplored the existence of the evil, as a great calamity and wrong; and they spoke as earnestly against it as any of the delegates from the northern states. This, the debates of that day abundantly show.—First and foremost among them, were such men as Thomas Jefferson, and James Madison; and in the first Congress that met, after the adoption of the Constitution, they took a leading part in framing and passing the celebrated ordinance of 1787, which declared, that slavery should be forever excluded from the vast north-west territory, which at that time embraced our whole national domain, outside of the old thirteen states, and there the matter rested, till the purchase of Louisiana, in 1801, which being already a slave state, was admitted into the Union, with metes and bounds, without any restriction or any resistance from the north. That purchase from France, extended beyond those limits, on the west side of the Mississippi, up to the British line. Here again, the question between slave and free territory rested, till 1819, when Missouri petitioned Congress for admission as a slave state, which for the first time, brought the north and south into open collision. The framers of the Constitution were dead, or too far advanced in age, to participate in the public counsels. Slavery had in the meantime taken deep root in the states south of the Potomac. Other rulers had arisen, "who knew not Joseph," and they determined, not only to hold on to the institution in their own Egypt, but to carry it along with them into Canaan. They contended, that as the whole territory, under the name of Louisiana, was the joint purchase of the free and slave states, they had a right to settle with their slaves upon whatever part of it they chose, and of course, that Missouri had a just claim to come in without any restrictions. On the other hand it was contended that the original understanding between their revolutionary fathers was, that slavery should never encroach upon any free territory, under the Federal government; that the territory out of which Missouri was carved, had no slaves in it at the time of the purchase, and that slavery had, and would have, no right to obtrude itself upon that free soil.

The contest on these grounds was long and earnest. Neither party would yield. The debates in Congress shook the whole nation and at one time seemed to threaten the dissolution of the Union. At length a compromise was made on the 17th of February, 1820, and the bill was carried through, chiefly by the powerful influence of southern men, as Mr. Sumner has just unanswerably shown, by names and dates, in his brilliant and powerful speech in the Senate, copies of which ought to be strown like the leaves of autumn, all over the free states. The explicit terms of this compromise on the side of freedom were, as I have already shown, that slavery was, and should be forever excluded from the territory north of 36 deg. 30 min. This was declared in Congress, by one of the most eminent jurists of the south, who had a principal agency in bringing it about, to be a COMPACT, which, as everybody understood it, was a final settlement of the question; and there it stood, just as much unquestioned FOR THIRTY-FOUR YEARS, as the plainest article in the Constitution itself. In the meantime, Arkansas, lying south of the compromise line, was admitted as a slave state without opposition, so that thus far, if the Nebraska bill passes, slavery has gained every thing out of the Louisiana purchase, and we nothing. Not satisfied with this, the slave power, ever sleepless and encroaching, next fixed its greedy eyes upon Texas, which had been violently rent off from the free republic of Mexico, and for fear of defeat and in spite of remonstrance, the bill of annexation was hurried through the House, almost with railroad speed, upon the last great amendment, which was, that the new state of Texas, might cut up that vast territory, into FOUR more slave states at her pleasure! If I am rightly informed, your own representative, was the only member that could get a chance to open his mouth in opposition, at that turning point. This was regarded on both sides, as a signal triumph of the slave power. Next came the Mexican war, not of course, AVOWEDLY, to add more slave territory ; but who can doubt that this was the great object of the men then in power. Thanks to a benevolent Providence, they have not yet succeeded, but you deceive yourselves, if you suppose, they have abandoned the hope. They never despair of anything in the line of slavery aggression, upon which they once set their hearts. Depend upon it, they will leave no means untried, to get a large slice to their own liking, from the conquered territory.

This brings down the history of aggression by our southern masters, to the present winter, and now we understand, that when the Nebraska bill comes from the Senate to the House, it is intended, by reviving the tactics which brought in Texas, to drive it through with breathless speed, trampling down in its passage, the national faith, and opening another vast free territory to the withering sirocco from the burning south. To the astonishment of the whole country, north and south, the exception of those who were in "the mystery of iniquity," they now march boldly up to the line of the Missouri Compromise, and having themselves already enjoyed the benefit of it for a third of a century, now just as we are entering upon the occupancy of our share of the joint estate, they claim the right of coming in at their convenience, and taking possession of a part or the whole of the remainder without our consent. And how are they to get over the line of 36 deg. 30 min., with their herds of human chattels ? Why, by annulling the compromise, to be sure. And why have they not done it before ? A whole generation has passed away since it was made. Why this strange tardiness of a whole life time, in asserting their rights ? Was it that they could not sooner get rid of some lingering qualms of conscience, against violating their solemnly plighted faith? Was it, that having more than half the farm on this side of the Rocky Mountains already in their possession, they did not want our share, till now? Was it because they were afraid they could'nt subsidise a sufficient number of our northern members of Congress, to help them? Or was it because they thought it most prudent to wait, till nearly all the men who made the compromise were dead, lest they should remonstrate and defeat them, as they most certainly would have done, a few years earlier?—Have they been kept back so long for all, or for any of these reasons?

If I understand them, they have two avowed objects in bringing forward the measure of repeal at this time. First to assert their right of occupancy with their slaves, quite up to the British line, and secondly, to put a final end to agitation.

With regard to the first of these objects, if it is a mere abstraction that they are contending for; if, as they say, they never expect to get slavery into Nebraska, and even do not want to, if they could, as some of them declare, what motive can they have in agitating the whole country, to repeal the compromise? It seems to me the leaders must be either unaccountably demented or insincere.

But the GRAND object which they avow is, to restore peace and brotherhood between the two great branches of our family, north and south, and to put an end to all further controversy. Now, I confess, that this is about the most remarkable way of settling a great and bitter quarrel, that I remember ever to have heard of in my long life. The "omnibus" compromise of 1850, which cost Mr. Clay his life, and another great man his political death, was claimed to be a FINALITY, that is, a final settlement of the slavery agitation, never more to be revived, in any form by the north or the south, "as long as the sun and the moon shall endure." And though it was not satisfactory in all its provisions to either side, the country seemed to be settling down upon it, as the best compromise perhaps that could be agreed upon. Now I wonder how many more FINALITIES, we at the north are to have forced upon us, by new aggressions. I do not understand how Mr. Douglas and his copartners expect to keep the body politic, sound, by exasperating old sores, which were pretty well scabbed over. I thought the safest way was, to let them alone. But now, it is all at once found out, in this age of new inventions, that the true, pathological way is, rudely to tear them open; to apply the scalpel to scars, which if not touched, would in time disappear, and to set them all bleeding again. This is a kind of surgery, for restoring to the body politic, soundness, which I believe has never till now, been taught in the schools. Not myself being one of the Faculty, I can't understand it. It looks to me just like what, if I do not mistake the term, they would in any other case call malpractice. At any rate, if my poor old body were to be laid upon the table, under a counsel of those northern and southern doctors, I should hope and pray that it might be a FINALITY.

Now, I undertake to say, that there is not an intelligent man, in his right mind, in the north or south, who will look candidly at the proposed healing measure, the Nebraska bill, who believes, or can believe that to push it through, can have any such effect.—

On the contrary, it is just as sure to create and inflame new agitations, as that the sun will rise to-morrow.

But if it were otherwise, how can anybody maintain, that the compromise of 1850, broke up, or in any way disturbed the compromise of 1820. So far as it settled any territorial question, between the south and the north, it had nothing in the world to do with the Missouri compromise ; and yet we are told in the papers, that the whole southern delegation will go for the bill, on this ground.

I do not believe it. How can they ? In the compromise so called, of 1850, the only question was, how shall we bring in and dispose of the new territory conquered from Mexico. It had no more reference to any other land, owned by the United States, than it had to so much surface of the planet Jupiter. Not a word, not a syllable was uttered during the long and stormy debates of 1850, having the remotest retrospective bearing upon the Missouri compromise of 1820. It was not alluded to ; it was not thought of by anybody, either in or out of Congress. If any such construction as is now contended for, had been hinted at, it would have killed the omnibus bill at a blow. Mr. Clay, and every other high-minded and honorable member from the south, would have denounced the insidious retrospective application in a moment.

Now, to say that the whole south in Congress, will endorse such a construction, I hold to be a libel upon their understanding, which all their friends ought indignantly to resent, and to believe it of them, requires a margin for their honesty, so wide, that we cannot afford it. I will try to show how it strikes me, and I believe will strike you, by a familiar illustration.

A company of twenty enterprising men, unite and purchase a large tract of wild land, in anticipation of future settlement. At length, ten of them want to take possession, and bring in a population of such a character, and introduce such a system of cultivation, as in the judgment of the other ten, would make a bad state of society, and greatly depreciate the value of the property. They can't consent to it, but their partners insist upon their right, on the score of joint ownership. High words follow. One party says you shan't bring in such a population, and the other says we will. At last, to settle the dispute, they agree upon a compromise, and both parties sign it. "We will divide the tract on such a line, east and west. If you want to burden yourselves with a class of settlers, who will be a curse to you, rather than contend about it any longer, you may do it on your side of the line, but you shall never bring one of them over, to settle on our side, neither you nor your heirs forever."

"Agreed," respond the other party, and the compromise is signed, sealed, and deposited in a safe place. The ten partners who had been most strenuous in making the agreement, go on, with such settlers as they like, and take possession. The other ten are not yet ready, and though they exceedingly regret that they are to have such troublesome neighbors, they do nothing to disturb the compromise. At length, they propose to remove and settle upon their new land, and to invite such imigrants as they like, to plant themselves down around them. In the mean time, the same company purchase another large tract, several hundred miles off. The same disagreement springs up there, and is settled by compromise as before, and there the matter rests for a great many years. When, Lo, and behold, without an hour's notice, the party that had already settled a mongrel population under the first compromise, make their appearance in force on the line, and demand the right, as original joint proprietors, of coming over. "No, we can't allow it," is the answer. We don't like such people as we see in your company. Have you forgotten the recorded contract, which forever excludes such settlers?

Oh no; but have YOU forgotten our more recent compromise, by which we divided that other large purchase, and which annulled the first on the strength of, which you now refuse us." "Annulled it! how, since it was not so much as alluded to, in our last purchase and division." "We can't stop to dispute with you about that," is the imperious reply. "It WAS repealed, whether you can see how or not. We have now as good a right as you have, to occupy any and every part of the first purchase, and we are determined to maintain it, whether you will or not. We have found these people whom you would shut out, excellent "hewers of wood and drawers of water," and we only wish we had more of them."

This, my friends, is precisely the logic by which, after having established slavery in Missouri, under the Compromise of 1820, the slave power now seeks to get possession of Nebraska. It is the perfidious violation of a solemn National compact, which, by party disciples, is to be trampled under foot by both houses of Congress. Did the fathers of the Republic imagine it possible, that it would ever come to this? Is one compromise with slavery, to make an earlier one for freedom void, with which the latter had nothing in the world to do, and the chivalry of the South to go in mass for it! The bill before Congress, for repealing the Missouri Compromise, which solicits all their votes, has been altered and amended so many times, by its responsible author, at the suggestion and to suit the friends of the measure, that it is difficult to say how it now stands; and impossible to predict, in what shape it will finally pass, if pass it must, which may righteous Heaven forbid! Look for a moment, and see, by what gradual and sinister approaches things have reached the present alarming crisis. A bill for the organization of Nebraska into a territory, was brought into Congress at the last session, without any clause to disturb the Missouri Compromise. It passed the House and was sent up to the Senate. It was then near the close of the session, and professedly for want of time to consider it, was laid upon the table. Whether it was arrested by an after thought, that it did not go far enough, I cannot undertake to say.

But the present bill came out boldly in the first draft, and declared that the Missouri Compromise of 1820, was ANNULLED by that of 1850. This phraseology not quite suiting some of the friends, it was amended, by substituting the word SUPERSEDED for ANNULLED. After debate, this was dropped, and the bill amended so as to read "The Missouri Compromise was rendered INOPERATIVE by that of 1850."—Even this, not fully satisfying all the coalition, Mr. Douglas told the Senate, previous to an adjournment, that the committee would take back the bill, and endeavor so to modify it, as to obviate every objection. How it stands now is more than I can tell you ; and it is no matter, provided always, that it does the work of killing off the Missouri Compromise, and letting in slavery.

A grand auto-da-fe, seems to be agreed upon in the Senate, and though there is some difference of opinion, as to wording the sentence of death, the principal Inquisitors, will not quarrel with one another about the mode of execution, whether it shall be by strangling, beheading, or drawing in quarters, provided the victim is forever put out of the way. Some of the executioners may be so tender-hearted as to relent, and wish to be excused in the last extremity, but they cannot be let off ; they must all prove their allegiance to the ruling power, by doing its bidding.

Let us, next, for a moment, inquire about the paternity of this bill, and from what section of the country it has found its way into the Senate. Did it come from the south, whose interest it is intended to favor, by opening a vast new territory for the extension of slavery ? No — the south are too "wise in their generation" for that. I do not believe that there is one Senator south of Mason and Dixon's line, who would have ventured to present it, for fear that such an acknowledged paternity would defeat the bill, as it most undoubtedly would have done. And if a southern administration had now been in power, and known to be committed to the measure, do you think the south would have ventured upon so bold and aggressive a step ? Most assuredly they would not, for they must have known it would rouse the free states at once, to successful resistance. Whenever the slave states have any such object to gain, they must very much wish, to have a northern man with southern principles in the Presidential chair, with that tremendous official patronage, which his position gives him. It allays suspicion in the free states, and gives the south an advantage, which they could not possibly have, were the chair filled by one of their own ablest men. This then is the time to take another long stride towards gaining that ascendency over us, at which they have been always aiming. A northern President is now at the head of the government and the majority of his Cabinet are from the free states.

But something further was necessary to insure the safety and passage of the bill. To make it go down, it must be brought in by some prominent free state Senator. Who should it be ? The man was readily found, who, I am sorry to say was born in New England, near the battle fields of Bennington and Saratoga, and right under the north star that never wavers. Thanks to a kind providence, he does not MISrepresent any one of our old Puritan states. It is surmised by some, I see, that upon the ladder of this Nebraska bill, he hopes to climb to the highest seat of power in this free country. Perhaps he may, but he has already shifted so many rounds of the ladder, that in spite of all his cabinate skill, it may prove too rickety to bear his weight. I think it will, before he gets half to the top ;—quite sure I am, that "the angels of God, will not be seen, either ascending or descending upon it.

And again, how is this bill to be carried through Congress ? In the usual way, when great public interests are involved ? No, but by a COUP D'ETAT, very much like that which so lately placed a usurper on the throne of France. Almost on the very day when the bill, like a clap of thunder in a clear sky, astounded every body not in the secret, Mr. Douglas expressed a hope that the question might be taken in the Senate, before the end of the week.—And what was the object of this hot haste, what could it be, but to spring the trap upon the free states before the people had time to express their opinions, or even to see the bill. I boldly say, this was the object.

And how is it to be carried through Congress, and break down the defences of freedom on the line of 36 deg. 30 min. ? Can the slave representatives do it, without the aid of the free north ? No, that were impossible. In the Senate, we have two majority, and in the House, FIFTY-FOUR. How then, can they expect to succeed ? I will tell you how. In all ordinary subjects of legislation, where party lines are drawn, the Whigs in the slave States, act with the Whigs in the free States, and so it is with the Democrats. They act together. But whenever any question arises between liberty and slavery, these party lines vanish in a moment, and the Sonth marches up to meet us in solid column. Whereas we are divided among ourselves. We must stick to our party at all hazards, "though the heavens should fall;" so that, when we meet them hand to hand a sufficient number of deserters from our ranks go over, to give them the victory. So it always has been. It is by our help, that they have carried every question against us, and gradually extended their encroachments upon liberty, ever since the contest between slavery and freedom began. They now confidently expect to carry the Nebraska bill by the same northern treachery. But will they, can they ? Everybody would declare it impossible, if we did not know what rewards they have to offer, and what patent screws they have to put on when need so requires, at Washington.

According to the last census, the population of the free states was, in round numbers, 13,000,000, while the free population of the slave states was only 6,000,000, a difference on the side of freedom of more than two to one.* I hazard nothing in saying, that if the whole North could be polled to-morrow, and there was no fear of the whip and spur, nineteen-twentieths of the votes would be cast against the Nebraska conspiracy. And I do not believe, that if the whole delagation of the free States now in Congress, could be brought home, to meet their constituents face to face, that aside from party discipline, a single man of them could be sustained in voting for that bill. If any of them do vote for it, it does not belong to me to prophecy, what will be their fate at the next election, but some of you remember the fate of your own representative from this County, who voted to receive Missouri into the Union as a slave state. But for that fatal step, such were his talents and popular address, that he might have stood a fair choice for the highest promotion in the State. If that Missouri vote had been a grape shot, aimed at his heart it would not have been more fatal to his political prospects. I take it for granted, that no representative from this our mountain district, will ever after venture so to MIS-represent his constituents, till he first settled up all his affairs for deliberate suicide.

And it is perfectly easy to teach any Northern man, who may be cajoled or brought over at the

---

*See the American Almanac, page 209, 1853.

present crisis, the same lesson, as soon as he gets home. To this end let me say, to all political parties, it is quite time for you to drop the names of Whigs and Democrats and Free Soilers, and march shoulder to shoulder, just as they do in all the slave states, on every question between liberty and slavery. In this way alone, can the further encroachments of the consolidated slave power be arrested. Keep up your political organizations for other purposes, if you must, but I beseech you not to betray the sacred cause of human freedom, by any longer allowing its enemies to divide and conquor you.

What they will not do next, if they can break down the Missouri Compromise by Northern votes, is hard to say; but the plot thickens. The storming of the still remaining outer defences of freedom, is to be followed up by still nearer approaches to the citadel. We learn from Washington, that at the very moment when Mr. Douglass was writing to New Hampshire, that there was no danger of slavery's ever getting into Nebraska, Mr. Orr of South Carolina was preparing a bill, for the establishment of slavery by Congress in that very territory. You will not believe it possible; but so it was. That bill, professedly intended to secure the rights of the Indian tribes in the territory, was last week brought into the House and ordered to be printed. It provides, that each family of these tribes may locate a homestead on the following terms:—"Each single person, over 21 years old, is entitled to eighty acres; each family of two persons 160 acres; each family of three and not over five, 320 acres; each family of six and not exceeding ten, 640 acres; and each family over ten 160 acres for every five members. AND TO FAMILIES WHO OWN SLAVES, IN ADDITION TO THE

FOREGOING, THERE SHALL BE ALLOWED, IF LESS THAN TEN SLAVES, ONE-HALF SECTION, (320 acres); IF TEN, NOT EXCEEDING FIFTEEN, ONE SECTION, (640 acres), AND FOR EVERY TEN ABOVE THAT NUMBER, ONE-HALF SECTION, (320 acres)!" This, according to slave logic, is only another necessary step, for carrying out the doctrine of NONINTERVENTION in the free territories! If it passes, I shall almost "despair of the republic." It will prove that our representatives are ready to surrender to the slave power all that is left to us, just as fast as it is wanted, and then it will be time to inquire whether we cannot bring back and refit the old May Flower, and embark with our wives and children on another stormy sea, in quest of some wilderness land, where we may again plant the tree of liberty and water it, if need be, as our fathers did, with our blood.

We were told when the Nebraska Bill was brought into the Senate, that it was an administration measure. Rendered into plain English this means, if you don't stand up to the bill and help carry it through, you must expect to be read out of the party, and to be cut off from getting any more of the loaves and fishes.

I confess, that this foreshadowing executive interference, presents to my mind the most alarming encroachment upon free unbiased legislation that has yet been developed. In theory the Federal Government consists of three independent and coordinate branches: the Executive, the Legislative and the Judicial. Our only safety, as a Republic, depends upon keeping them separate. The framers of the Constitution, never intended that one should control or interfere with the others.

But what have we now come to? The most important measure that has been proposed, since the adoption of the Constitution, is to be carried by a most alarming encroachment upon Legislative indedence. If the present conspiracy prevails, by means of Executive patronage, how long will it be, before the exercise of that now growing power will overshadow and control both the other branches of the Government.

Do you say, that this kind of interference with legislation in Congress is no new thing? It only increases my alarm. It shows it to be only carrying out a system of encroachments, which has been acted upon, till it has reached the present alarming crisis. When the Constitution was adopted, many of the wisest men in the nation feared, that the Executive branch would be overpowered and controlled by the Legislative. It could never have occurred to them what power they had put into the hands of the President, by giving him the appointment and nomination of officers from the highest to the lowest, to represent us abroad and fill all the places of trust and profit at home. Could they rise from the dead, they would be astonished to find how much they were mistaken; how overshadowing that power has already become. It is increasing alarmingly every year, and if the Union should hold together another quarter of a century, we have every reason to fear, it will become so gigantic that nothing can stand before it.

It is curious to notice, in looking over the debates in the Senate, how the advocates of the Nebraska bill have been driven from one position to another, till, as the last resort they have planted themselves upon the constitution. They intend to vote for the repeal of the Missouri Compromise because it is UNCONSTITUTIONAL. In answer to this, it were enough to say, that some of the ablest Jurists in the country, have over and over again pronounced it constitutional, when there was no pending question, to bias their judgments. If things progress at the present rate, how long will it be before half the constitution itself, will be declared UN-constitutional?

This government must have a moral basis to rest upon; it must adhere to its solemn compacts, or it cannot stand. Once let the public conscience be so perverted and seared, that the public faith of this great nation, can be trampled down by Congress, or any other power, with impunity, and it will be a sure presage that the government in its present form is in the last stage of decline. Let the Missouri Compromise be repealed and it will be the last between the free and slave states. Whatever crises may hereafter arise, requiring concessions and compacts, no such thing can be thought of. We cannot hold together as a nation without compacts. They lie at the foundation of our republic; the sappers and miners are at work. The edifice totters, and "if the foundation be destroyed, what can the righteous do?" Nay, what can the sappers and miners themselves do? If they succeed they will be buried with us under the ruins.

Pass that iniquitous bill now in its progress through Congress, and it will kindle a flame which all the waters of the Mississippi cannot put out.

But "why struggle any longer against a measure, which the Senate, backed up by the Administration, seem determined to push through, at all hazards? Why not give the matter rest, and let the Compromise go, rather than prolong the contest, especially as there is so little probability that slavery will ever gain a foothold in Nebraska, though the Missouri compact should be broken and annulled ?" I answer, depend upon it, the South would not contend so vehemently, and with such imperious brow-beating, for the mere abstract right of taking her negroes over the line, if she had no intention of passing it. She wants the territory to insure her political supremacy forever. She knows very well, that there is nothing in the climate to keep her out, for slavery can and does exist and increase in Missouri, most of which lies higher north than the south part of Nebraska. And there may be another reason for her spasmodic efforts, to get possession, which of course she dare not avow, and which I have not seen menned. If this bill passes, it will open to the South immense new BREEDING grounds. Why, it is one of the finest climates in the world, for raising black and grizzled live stock for the southern shambles, just as Virginia now does, and finds it much more profitable, than cultivating her worn-out soil.

And here, let us look for a moment at the extent of the territory, which they would fain wrest from us and doom everlastingly to the curse of slavery. It covers an area of 480,000 square miles, stretching over eleven and a half degrees of latitude, up to the British parallel of forty-nine, and west to the Rocky Mountains. It is SEVEN times larger than New England; and much larger than all the old thirteen States put together. It is TEN times larger than New York, with a population now of more than 3,000,000; and it might be cut up into sixty States as large as Massachusetts, which numbers 1,000,000. So you see there is room enough in that single territory, for a population of 60,000,000 of freemen, without making it denser than that of our own glorious Commonwealth, at this time.

And now, shall the solemn compact which has stood unquestioned thirty-four years, as a barrier against the further extension of slavery in that quarter, be broken down to let in the black and desolating torrent, and that by Northern votes! (for it cannot be done without them.) The final vote on the Nebraska bill, will decide, as far as human foresight can reach, whether new territory, large enough for an Empire, shall be consecrated to freedom, justice and humanity, to all generations, or whether the pall which already shrouds half the land, shall spread its black folds over all this wide and fair domain, also, up to the springs of Missouri. It is, whether free soil shall be protected any where, from the all-grasping encroachments of our Southern masters.

If the bill passes, what is to hinder then from scaling the Rocky Mountains, and taking possession of that vast fertile slope, on the other side, which looks away to where the sun goes down in the broad Pacific?

"Why not let them do it?" Does any one, who dares to call his soul his own, ask why not? Just for a moment bring the two systems of freedom and slavery together face to face. Let him look first at the one and then at the other, and if his conscience does not choke him, let him ask us why. If Nebraska remains the undisputed home of freedom, then it will be overspread by a vast industrious population, free as the air they breathe; and with their own strong arms turning the wilderness into a fruitful field. Then, like New England, it will be dotted all over with churches and schools and colleges and retreats for the insane, the blind, the mute, and the unfortunate of every class. Then will the poorest as well as the richest, be protected in the enjoyment of all their social, civil and religious rights. Under the smiles of heaven, great and prosperous States will spring up. Water and steam will do the work of more millions, in all branches of manufacturing and mechanical industry, than the Autocrat of all the Russias can number in his Empire. The Gospel will be preached in ten thousand pulpits, throughout that vast domain; heaven will smile upon all its free and glorious institutions, and as the millennial dawn opens and "shines more and more," songs of salutation will make the arches of the sky ring with the joy of numbers almost numberless, uninterrupted by the wailings of a single slave.

But, on the other hand, slavery, if it gets possession of Nebraska, will bring along with it, its bloody code of laws; its handcuffs; its scourages; its dogs for hunting down runaways; its licentiousness, against which slaves have no protection; its brutal ignorance; its hard bondage; its unrequited toil; its refusal of the holy sanctions of the marriage covenant; the rending at will of all the ties of natural affection; the slave pens where churches and school-houses and hospitals ought to stand; the slave traders, buying up all the black cattle they can find, at the lowest prices, for transportation to the rice swamps and cotton fields.

And, O! then will be heard the shrieks of distracted mothers, as their children are torn from their arms and sold into everlasting bondage; the sobbing of the poor creatures, men and women, who would have been husbands and wives if the law would let them, sold like brute beasts, and separated forever!

But I forbear. "My soul is sick." I cannot look at the picture without horror; I am sure all your sympathies are with me in this matter. But you ask, "What can we do? We are but few, away off here among these mountains, and the power is in hands entirely beyond our reach." Surely, what can we do?—but there is never a crisis, in which we cannot do something. When the Government was about driving away the Choctaws and Cherokees from their homes and their father's sepulchers, happening to meet that noble-hearted Christian philanthropist, Jeremiah Evarts, I asked him what we could do for our poor red brethren in their extremity. "What can we do," was his answer, "We can go out into the streets and cry murder."

Blessed be God, this is not all we can do, at the present critical juncture. There is a power, above all human combinations and encroachments, to which we can appeal. We can pray, as Daniel did, to the God of heaven, to turn back our captivity and save us. However lightly the slave power, now in Congress, may think of such an appeal, it is one which has been "mighty through God to the pulling down of strong holds."

There is and always has been a power in effectual, fervent prayer, which takes hold of Omnipotence, and has a thousand times prevailed against craft and violence. Mary Queen of Scotts, was heard to say that she was more afraid of John Knox's prayers than of 10,000 rebels in military array. And well she might be, for he "had power with God," and prevailed. Prayer is a sure resort in times of imminent peril. If all the people in the free States who have an interest at the throne of Grace, who love justice and "hate robbery," would cry mightily unto God in their public assemblies, in their families, and in their closets, at this crisis, I have no doubt the Nebraska bill would be defeated.

It is well known, I believe, that in the technical sense of the term, I am no abolitionist. I wish I could say the same of Mr. Douglass, and those who act with him, but I cannot help regarding men who would break down the defences of free territory, as the most dangerous ABOLITIONISTS in the country. I hate slavery, with all my heart, and pray God that it may never gain another foot of land on this continent.

While this iniquitous bill is pending, I say remonstrate, protest, agitate to the last hour. Had I strength adequate to the task, I would go out and plead against it, wherever I could gain a hearing; but my old voice is almost worn out. "The wheel is too near being broken at the cistern." I call upon you that are younger to ascend to every hill top, and blow the trumpet of freedom long and loud.

This is eminently a great moral and religious question, in its bearings upon all coming generations. It sinks party politics entirely out of sight. If I had a hundred voices, and could make them reach all the thousands of my clerical brethren in the land, I would earnestly ask, "Who knoweth but that you are come to the stations which you occupy, for such a time as this?" Can you refrain from publicly remonstrating against the great wrong and danger of violating the public faith solemnly pledged in the Missouri Compromise, and opening an almost boundless new territory for the entrance and spread of slavery? There cannot be a question what our fathers of '76, in the ministry would do if they were on the stage, and shall we not prove ourselves worthy to be called their sons?

www.ingramcontent.com/pod-product-compliance
Lightning Source LLC
LaVergne TN
LVHW011133110826
845150LV00008B/2331

* 9 7 8 1 4 1 8 1 9 4 0 2 4 *